A GUIDE TO SAN DI

Written & Illustrated by Nancy Lee
www.nldesignsbythesea.com

Copyright @2016 Nancy Lee

All rights reserved.
No part of this book may be reproduced without the consent of the author.

ISBN – 13: 978-1535150415

ISBN – 10: 1535150416

www.nldesignsbythesea.com

nancyleeartbythesea@gmail.com

All of the watercolors in this book have been illustrated & painted from sea shells that I have collected on San Diego beaches. The sea shell photographs at the back of this book were photographed on paintings of eel grass with information about the shells written in calligraphy. I have returned many of the sea shells used for these illustrations & photographs back to the sea.

I started learning the names of sea shells when I was at a beach in La Jolla and another shell collector took a few minutes to show me sea shells & tell me their names. Ever since learning that a tiny brown cowry shell was called a Coffee Bean shell I have been interested in learning more about the sea shells on our San Diego beaches and in our tide pools.

While researching San Diego sea shells for this book, I was surprised to discover how long some shells live and how sea shells both living & empty create a healthy environment for our ocean, tide pools & beaches. I hope that you find this book about San Diego sea shells interesting, fun & informative.

Nancy Lee
Artist By-the-Sea
2016

San Diego Scallop

Pecten diegenis dall.

"Butterfly" Scallop

Bodega Bay, California to Baja California.

Scallop motif is found on Spanish Missions in California. Scallop shell symbols mark Pilgrim's route.

N. LEE

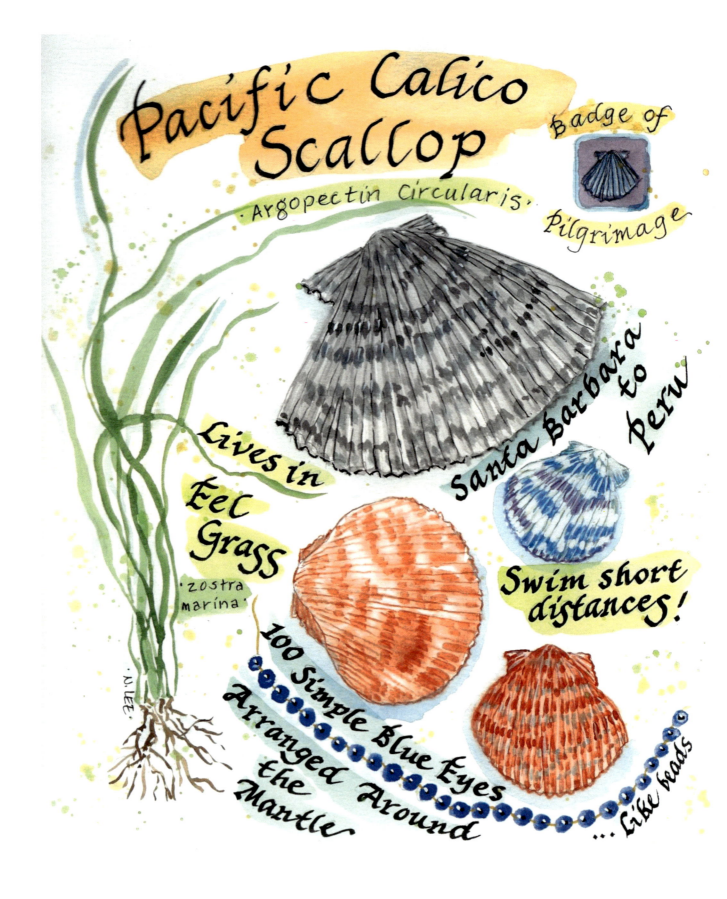

Eccentric Sand Dollar

- *dendraster excentricus*
- sea urchin class

"Sea Cookie" in New Zealand

Alaska to Baja California

Back ↰

Wash ashore white

- Related to:
  - Sea urchins
  - Sea cucumbers
  - Starfish

Live 6-10 years

Lives in dense beds

Predators:
- California Sheepheads
- Starry flounder
- Large Pink Sea Stars

Purple or green velvet-textured spines/cilia when alive

Giant Acorn Barnacle

Balanus nubilis

Alaska to San Diego

Looks like a tiny volcanic crater

Feathery legs to feed on plankton

Live on rocks, pilings & hard-shelled invertebrates

Volcano Limpet

Fissurella volcano.

Keyhole Limpet Family

Aquatic Snail

· Less than 1" ·

From Crescent City, California to Baja California

· Predators Starfish, Fish, Seals & Shore Birds

· Lives more than 10 years ·

Reddish purple streaks on shell look like lava flowing from a crater.

N. LEE

- Sea Snail

Chestnut Cowrie

- Cypraea Spadicea
- Monterey, California to Baja
- Used as money
- Lives under rocks
- Worn as protection · Ocean Strength

California Frog Shell

bursa california

Scavenger often found in lobster traps

From: Monterey, California
To: Baja

Kellett's Whelk
·Kelletia kelletii·

Large Sea Snail

3" - 6 ½"
A 3 ½" whelk is 20 years old.

Feeds on turban snails, giant sea stars, & dead lobsters, squid & fish.

Predators: Octopus, otters, sea stars, Moon Snails, Horn Sharks & man.

From: Monterey, California
To: Central Baja California

N. LEE

Wavy Turban

megastraea undosa

feeds on algae

sea snail marine mollusk

Pt. Conception, California to Central Baja

Japanese delicacy "Sazae"

"Sazae-oni" is a Japanese shell fish ogre resembling a large 30 year old turban snail.

Norris's Top Snail

AKA: Smooth Brown Turban or Kelp Sea Snail

- gastropod mollusk
- *norrisia norrisii*
- Empty shells used by hermit crabs
- Pt. Conception, California to Baja California
- Fawn colored, greenish inside
- Feeds on Kelp
- Predators: sea stars, California Spiny Lobsters, Octopus & Otters

N. LEE

Purple Dwarf Olive Shell

- *olivella biplicata*
- marine snail

Burrows in sand

- Lives 8-15 years
- Eats kelp

Vancouver Island, British Columbia to Baja California Mexico

Bead Money "Anchum"

*Channel Islands
*Chumash Native Americans

Used as decorative beads for 9,000 years

*"seashell people"

N. LEE

Eroded Periwinkle
littorina keenae

Alaska to Baja California

Lives 5-10 years

Uses band of horny teeth to scrape algae from rocks

Ancient food source in Europe

Giant Western Nassa
nassarius fossatus

AKA: (channeled Dog Whelk)

AKA: (Basket Shell)

British Columbia to Baja California

Scavenger feeds on small clams

predators: giant pink sea star

"S" is for San Diego Sea Shells

The following pages are of San Diego sea shells, which were photographed on eel grass paintings. Information about the sea shells was written in calligraphy on the paintings.

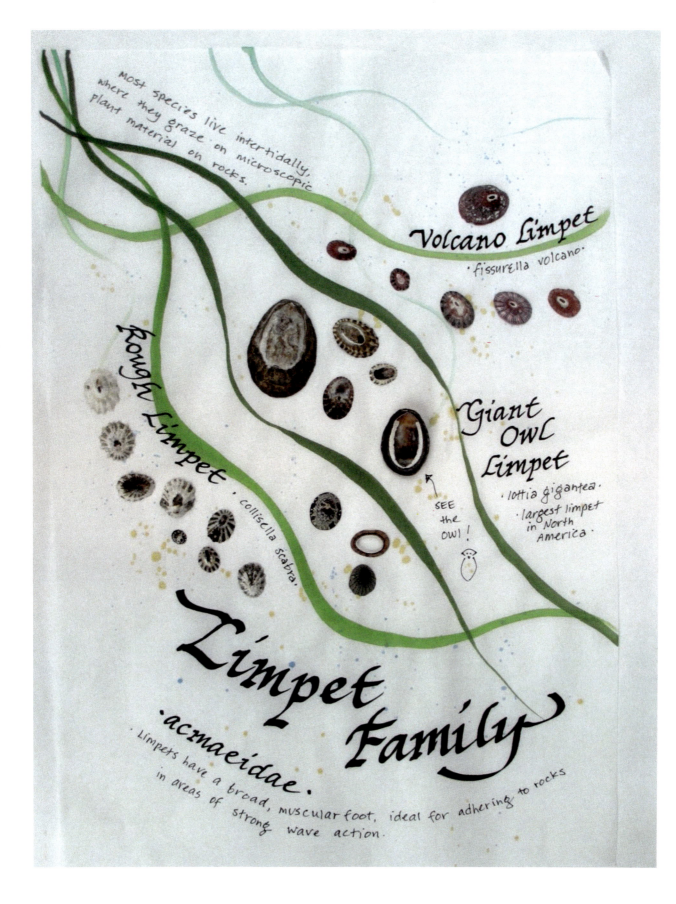

Sea Shell "Collecting"

- Photograph shells on the beach
- Carry a sketchbook & draw the shells you find
- Leave shells on the beach because they are an important part of our sea shore environment

"Take nothing, leave nothing"

N. LEE

Made in the USA
San Bernardino, CA
19 July 2020